This book belongs to

_____

Paperback ISBN: 978-1-63731-578-1
Hardcover ISBN: 978-1-63731-580-4

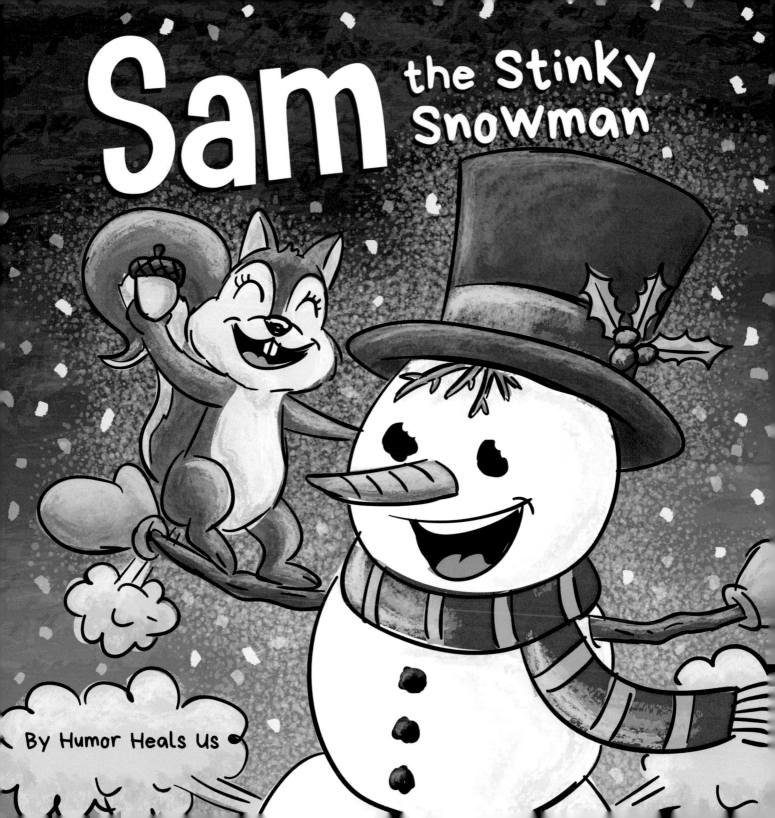

Sam the Stinky Snowman

the Stinky Snowman

By Humor Heals Us

Once upon a winter snowfall,
On the edge of a village where the trees grow tall,
In between houses on a patch of barren land,
<u>T</u>here lived Sam, the stinky snowman.

Why was he stinky, dare you ask?
Because Sam had smelly, uncontrollable gas.
It was the most awful scent anyone had ever smelled,
And somehow his gas did not seem to make him melt.

While Sam was embarrassed about his smelly toots,
They weren't just stinky— they were strong enough to shake his boots!
They would thunder and roar as Sam let them out.
His toots shook the ground as he waddled about.

But his stinkies were not ONLY smelly and quaking,
The kind of boots that would leave the earth shaking,
They were also, incredibly, audibly LOUD!
When Sam snuck one out, he certainly was not proud.

For when he did, the snowman would start to blush,
And do you know what a blushing snowman looks like? MUSH!
Not quite melted water like you see in the bath,
But that squishy, gushy stuff that leaves a trail in your walking path.

He would not only blush, he would whimper and whine.
He did not understand why this happened to him all the time.
For of all the people, creatures and friends he would meet,
This didn't happen to them, he said, "Why only ME?"

One day, Sam had to go into town.
He had shopping to do and no one was around.
That's right, he waited until a time the crowd would be gone,
So he could shop without worry and let out a backside song.

The day was going well as he bought cookies and bread.
When all of a sudden, Sam felt something on his head.
As soon as he did, he felt a rumble in his butt
As he looked to the ground and saw a small walnut.

"OUCH! That hurt!" the snowman said,
Sore and confused about how the nut fell on his head.
"HEY! UP HERE!" Sam heard from the roof,
And he saw a small squirrel saying, "Woof, woof!"

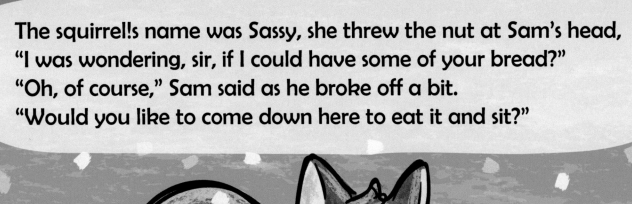

The squirrel!s name was Sassy, she threw the nut at Sam's head,
"I was wondering, sir, if I could have some of your bread?"
"Oh, of course," Sam said as he broke off a bit.
"Would you like to come down here to eat it and sit?"

Sassy gathered her belongings and swiftly came down.
She told Sam all about why she came into town.
"I was running away so I could hide.
You see, Sam, I have an embarrassing secret inside."

Sam didn't want to press but he wanted to know.
He was sure he'd find out Sassy's secret before he had to go.
And just as he thought it, she started to blush,
And the edge of Sam's snow belly began to mush.

He recognized what was happening as Sassy started to scoot.
The squirrel, she was letting out a STINKY TOOT!
It was loud and ground-shaking, more than for a squirrel you would think.
And you know what else? You bet it did stink!

Sam told Sassy, "No worries, it's okay."
"Oh, Sam," Sassy said. "That is such a kind thing to say."
Sam told her that the same happened to him all the time,
And together, the two decided pooting is NOT a crime!

The new friends proudly made their way through town,
No longer worrying who or what was around.
And if one—or both—of them let out a little gas,
They would turn to each other, smile and laugh.

Follow us on FB and IG @humorhealsus
To vote on new title names and freebies, visit
us at humorhealsus.com for more information.

@humorhealsus   @humorhealsus

Made in the USA
Middletown, DE
06 December 2024

66281180R00022